What are...?

CAVES

Claire Llewellyn

For more information about Heinemann Library books, or to order, please telephone +44 (0)1865 888066, or send a fax to +44 (0)1865 314091. You can visit our web site at www.heinemann.co.uk

First published in Great Britain by Heinemann Library,
Halley Court, Jordan Hill, Oxford OX2 8EJ
a division of Reed Educational and Professional Publishing Ltd.
Heinemann is a registered trademark of Reed Educational & Professional Publishing Ltd.

OXFORD MELBOURNE AUCKLAND
JOHANNESBURG BLANTYRE GABORONE
IBADAN PORTSMOUTH (NH) USA CHICAGO

Designed by David Oakley
Illustrations by Hardlines (p.13) and Jo Brooker
Printed by South China Printing Co.(1988) Ltd, Hong Kong / China

05 04 03 02 01
10 9 8 7 6 5 4 3 2 1

ISBN 0 431 02385 9

British Library Cataloguing in Publication Data
This book is also available in a hardback library edition (ISBN 0 431 02377 8)

Llewellyn, Claire
What are caves?
1. Caves – Juvenile literature
1. Title II. Caves
551.4'47

Acknowledgements
The Publishers would like to thank the following for permission to reproduce photographs: Bruce Coleman: p.29; Ecoscene: Rob Nichol p.9, Sally Morgan p.12; FLPA: John Bastable p.8, W Wisniewski p.10, Terry Whittaker p.11, Chris Demetriou p.17; NRSC/Airphoto Group: Forestry Commission p.22, p.24; Oxford Scientific Films: Alastair Shay p.4, Kim Westerskov p.6, Martyn Chillmaid p.7, Mills Tandy p.14, JAL Cooke p.19, T Middleton p.20; Robert Harding Picture Library: AC Waltham p.15, MPH p.16, Richard Ashworth p.28; Still Pictures: D Escartin p.18; Telegraph Colour Library: Masterfile p.5, Jean Marc Blache p.21; White Scar Caves: p.26.

Cover photograph reproduced with permission of Robert Harding Picture Library.

Every effort has been made to contact copyright holders of any material reproduced in this book. Any omissions will be rectified in subsequent printings if notice is given to the Publisher.

Contents

Some words are shown in bold, **like this**. You can find out what they mean by looking in the Glossary.

What is a cave?

A cave is a place where rock has worn away to leave a hollow space under the ground or in a hillside.

This cave has been made under the ground.

This cave has been made under the sea.

There are caves all over the world. They are found along the coast, under the ground and in the sides of mountains and hills.

Making sea caves

The sea is very powerful. All along the coast, strong waves batter the cliffs. Over many years the sea wears away the rock.

Day after day, the sea crashes against the foot of the cliff.

The foot of this cliff has been worn away.

The sea eats into the bottom of the cliff. If there is a weak part in the rock, the sea can start to make a hole in the bottom of the cliff.

How sea caves grow

The sea has made caves
in these rocky cliffs.

In some places, the bottom of a cliff begins to crack. The cracks are made bigger and bigger by the sea. Slowly, the cracks are made into caves.

Sea-water shoots up through a **blow-hole** in the roof of a cave.

Some sea caves have cracks in the roof. The sea crashes against the cracks. In time, this makes a hole called a blow-hole.

Making an arch

Two sea caves sometimes meet back-to-back, as the rock between them is worn away. This makes an **arch** in the rock.

An arch is made when two caves meet.

These pillars of rock are on the coast of Australia.

Over many years, the roof of the arch is worn away. It falls down into the sea. This leaves a pillar of rock standing up in the sea. This is called a **stack**.

Underground caves

Caves are sometimes found underground. They are almost always found in places where the rock is made of **limestone**.

These hills are made of limestone. There are caves under them.

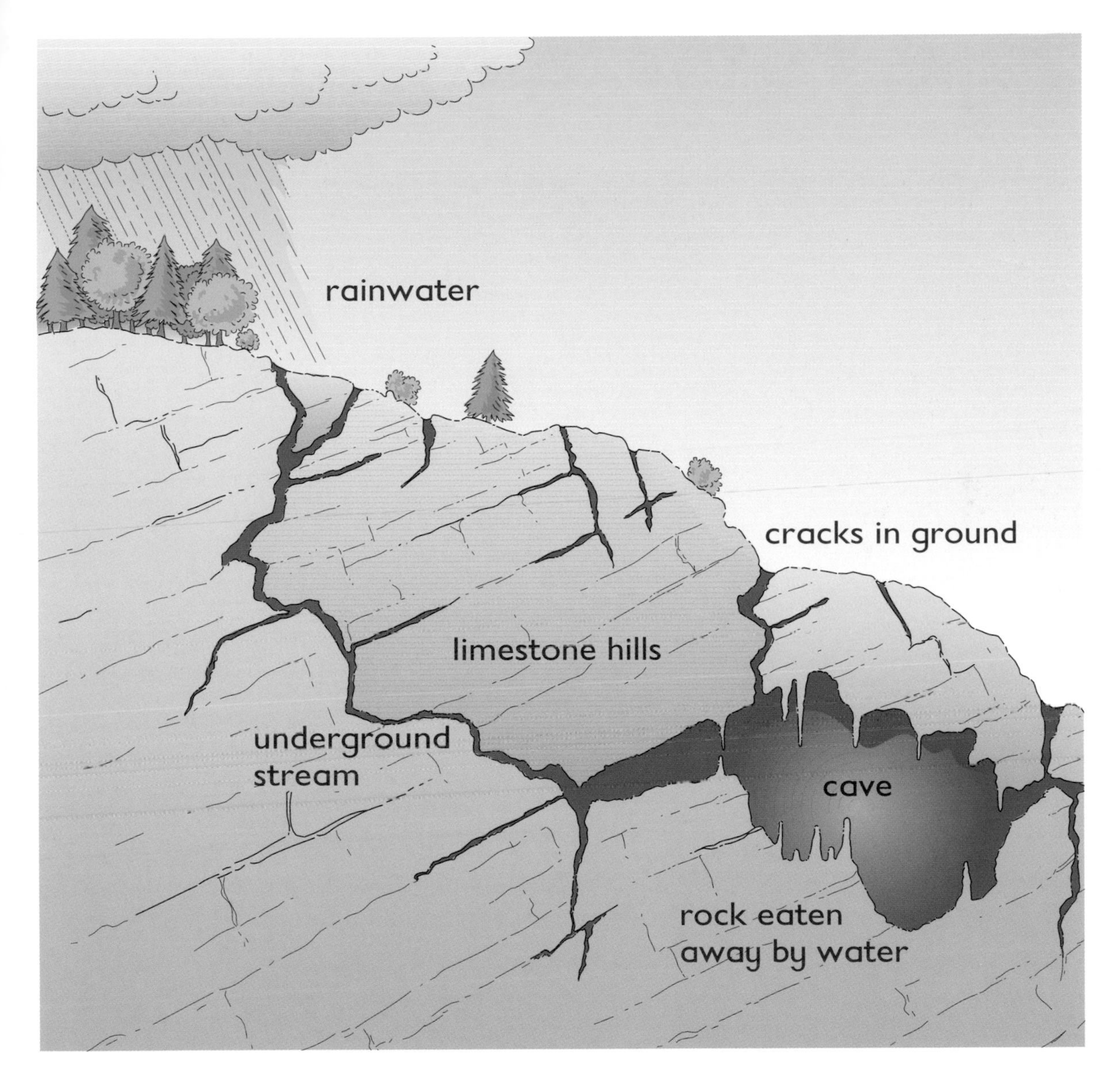

Limestone is **dissolved** by rainwater. The water trickles down through cracks in the ground, and slowly wears away the rocks below. Eventually a cave is made.

The cave grows

This huge cave has been made by water flowing underground.

Over thousands of years, underground streams **dissolve** the **limestone**. Cracks in the rock grow bigger and bigger until they make huge tunnels and caves.

People can only visit this cave in a boat!

Some underground caves and tunnels are flooded with water. Others are dry.

In the cave

Strange rock shapes can grow in some caves.

The drops of water that trickle underground contain tiny pieces of **limestone**. Some of the drops dry up as they fall, and leave the tiny rock pieces behind. These pile up inside caves.

Fingers of rock hang from the roof of a cave. They are called **stalactites**. Pillars of rock grow up from the floor of a cave. They are called **stalagmites**.

Stalactites and stalagmites grow very slowly over thousands of years.

Hill caves

People made these drawings in this cave in Algeria thousands of years ago.

Caves are made in mountains and hills by the wind, wet weather and running water. They have been used for shelter for thousands of years.

In some places, shepherds still use caves to shelter their sheep. Many wild animals, such as bats, use caves for shelter, too.

Bats rest in caves by day and go out to feed at night.

Exploring caves

People who study caves are called **speleologists**. They study the rocks and draw maps of the tunnels and caves.

These speleologists are studying an underground tunnel.

These men are wearing **protective** clothing in this flooded tunnel.

Exploring caves can be dangerous because they are sometimes flooded when it rains. To be safe, speleologists often take diving gear and boats.

Cave map 1

This photo was taken by an aeroplane. You can see high **limestone** hills. Between the hills, you can see a river and a road. You can also see two **quarries** by the road.

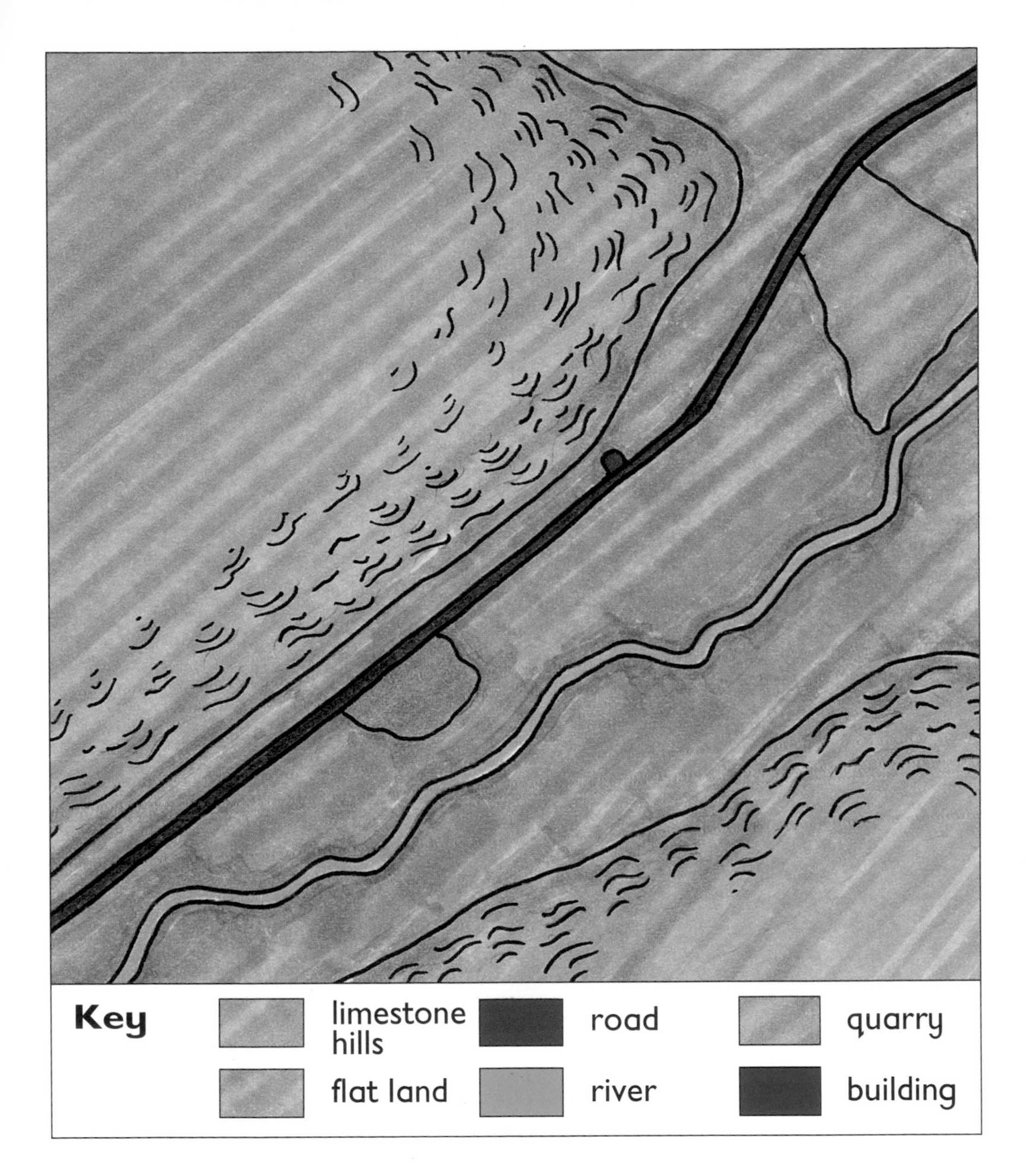

Maps are pictures of the land. This map shows us the same place as the photo. The key tells us what each colour means. The brown colour shows the hills. The green colour shows the flat land.

Cave map 2

This photo shows a smaller part of the land, but you can see it more clearly. You can see some buildings along the road. One of the buildings is the entrance to caves. The caves are under the hills.

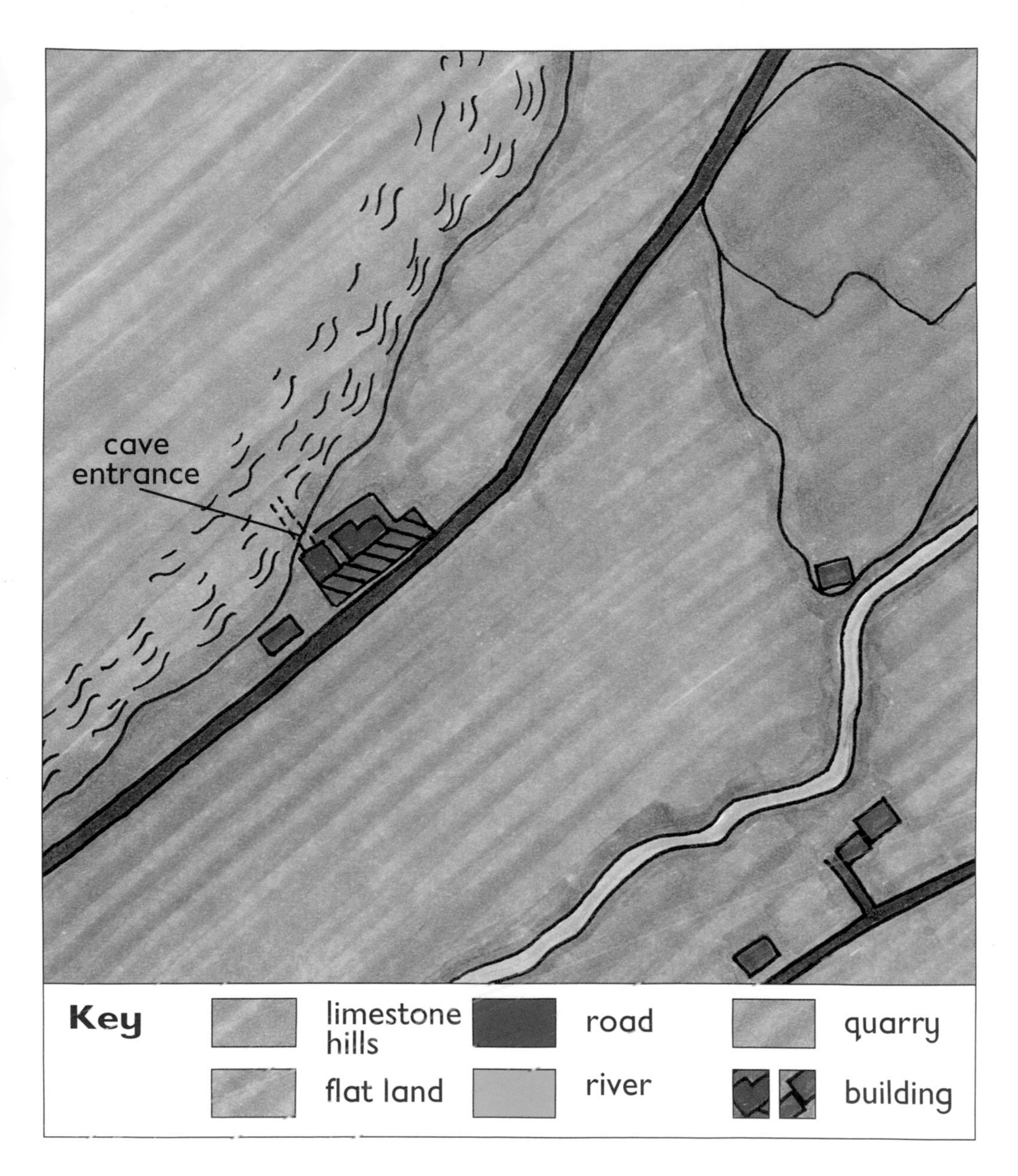

Maps give people useful information. This map shows how to get to the caves. It shows the buildings at the entrance of the caves in red. The black stripes show visitors where to park their cars.

Cave map 3

This photo shows one of the underground caves. It is called Battlefield Cavern. The cave has many **stalactites**. People reach it by an underground tunnel.

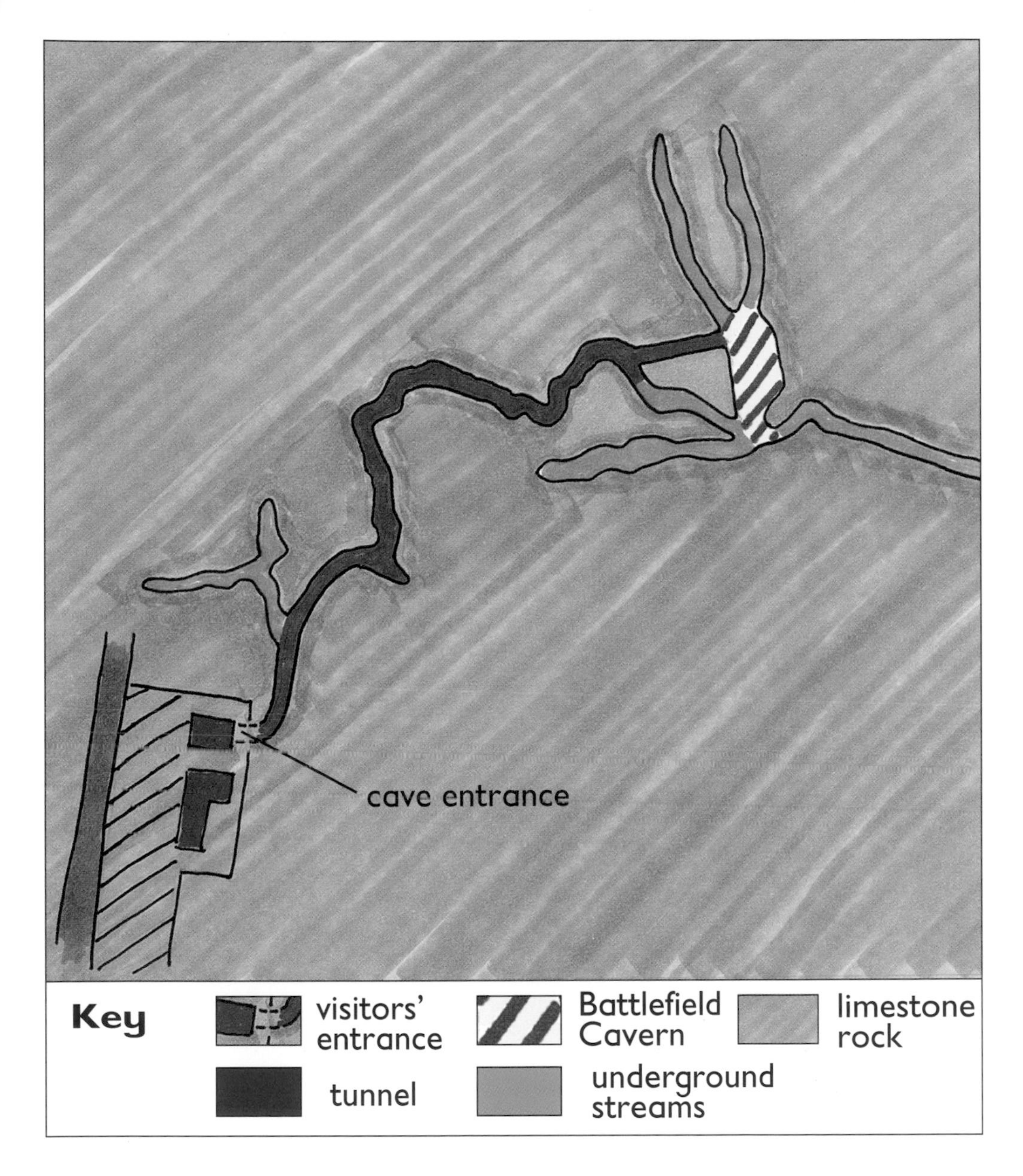

This map shows the way from the cave entrance to Battlefield Cavern. The purple colour shows the underground tunnel. Some tunnels have streams in them. The **limestone** rocks are coloured brown.

Amazing cave facts

The world's largest cave is the Sarawak Chamber on the island of Borneo. It would have room for about 800 tennis courts inside it!

The Mammoth Cave National Park in Kentucky, USA, contains caves that stretch for over 560 kilometres – about the distance between London and Edinburgh.

Glossary

arch a curved piece of rock on top of two pillars

blow-hole a hole in the roof of a cave. Sea-water gushes up through the hole.

dissolve to disappear in water, like sugar in tea

limestone a kind of rock that dissolves in rainwater

protective to keep people safe

quarry a place where sand or stone is dug out of the ground

speleologist a person who studies caves

stack the pillar of rock left standing in the sea when an arch falls down

stalactite a finger of rock that grows down from the roof of a cave

stalagmite a pillar of rock that grows up from the floor of a cave

More books to read

Steven Kramer.
Caves. Lerner Publishing, 1995

Donald M. Silver and Patricia J. Wynne.
One Small Square: Cave.
Learning Triangle Press, 1997

Index